Contents

LIBRARIES NI
WITHDRAWN FROM STOCK

Adélie Penguin

More than two million Adélie penguins live in Antarctica and islands nearby. Parents use stones to build their nests, and they both take care of the chicks.

Arctic Fox

When it is cold outside, Arctic fox
cubs stay cosy inside their burrow.
On warm days, they come out to play.
Arctic foxes grow brown coats in the
summer, but in the snowy winter a
white coat helps them to hide.

7

Brown Bear

Bear babies are very big babies! They are called cubs and they sleep in dens when it is very cold. Bear cubs like to roll in the snow, and explore their forest home.

8

Snow lays thick on the ground, and there is not much food to eat in the winter. This mother bear ate plenty of berries and roots in the summer, so she could store up layers of fat under her fur. She feeds her cubs with milk.

Dall's Sheep

It can be very cold at the top of a mountain, where Dall's sheep live. Sometimes, there is still snow on the mountain tops in summer. A mother sheep is called a ewe, and her baby is called a lamb. The lamb climbs, runs and jumps along the rocks.

Emperor Penguin

The Antarctic is the coldest place on Earth, where winter lasts for six months. Life is hard, but millions of penguins make their homes there. Emperor penguin babies are called chicks. They hatch out of their eggs in the middle of winter.

The mother walks to the sea to fetch fish. It is two months before she returns. The father looks after the chick. He holds it on his feet, so it doesn't freeze on the ice. The chick is grey and fluffy, but it will grow black and white feathers by the summer, when it is time to go swimming.

17

Fallow Deer

Little fallow deer fawns are always looking and listening for danger. They can move quickly when they are scared. Fawns have brown fur with white spots. When the spring comes, they will sit under bushes or trees and hide.

18

19

Harp Seal

Harp seals spend most of their time swimming in the icy Arctic Ocean. They have thick layers of fat, and fur, to keep them warm. Baby seals are called pups and they have white fur.

A pup cannot swim until it has grown a new coat of dark fur. It gets very hungry while it is waiting for the new fur to grow. This pup is waiting for its mother to dive into the water and find some crabs and fish to eat.

23

24

Husky

Huskies are clever and friendly animals. They are fast runners, and they love to play chase in the snow. Huskies are Arctic dogs that live where the winters are very long and icy-cold winds blow. They live in groups, called packs, and huddle up together to keep warm.

King Penguin

King penguins lay their eggs in the spring and look after their chicks in the summer, but it is still cold and snowy! These water-loving birds live near the South Pole.

26

King penguin chicks don't look like their
mum or dad. They have round, brown fluffy
bodies and they are called 'woolly penguins'.
While their parents go off to hunt for fish,
the chicks huddle together
to stay warm.

29

Mountain Goat

Mountain goats climb up hills and cliffs to hide from bears, wolves and mountain lions. Even baby goats, also known as kids, can skip through the snow without slipping. Mountain goats eat plants, and they nibble on snow when they are thirsty.

30

31

Mountain Lion

The snow is deep, but a cute mountain lion cub doesn't mind! Cubs start to play when they are ten days old. They practise pouncing, chasing and hiding. Mountain lions are also called pumas.

33

34

Muskox

Muskox families spend the whole year in the Arctic, even the freezing winter months when there is little grass to eat. The adults take good care of their calves and protect them from wolves and bears.

Panda Bear

A panda bear cub is so tiny when it is born that it weighs the same as an apple. Soon, it is big enough to play outside in the snow. Giant pandas climb trees and eat bamboo.

36

Polar Bear

Little cubs keep an eye open for danger. When they are bigger, they will be fearless. Polar bears live in the Arctic and they love the snow. Their fur is so thick that in the summer they can get too hot!

40

Polar bears are the world's biggest bears. Mum builds her cubs a den so they are born in a warm, safe place. In the spring, the fluffy cubs come out of the den to explore and learn how to hunt.

Red Fox

Little red fox cubs are often born before the spring sunshine comes. Their mother keeps them snug inside her den while they grow strong. Soon, they can leave their home to play outside. If they get too chilly or wet, they go back inside to warm up.

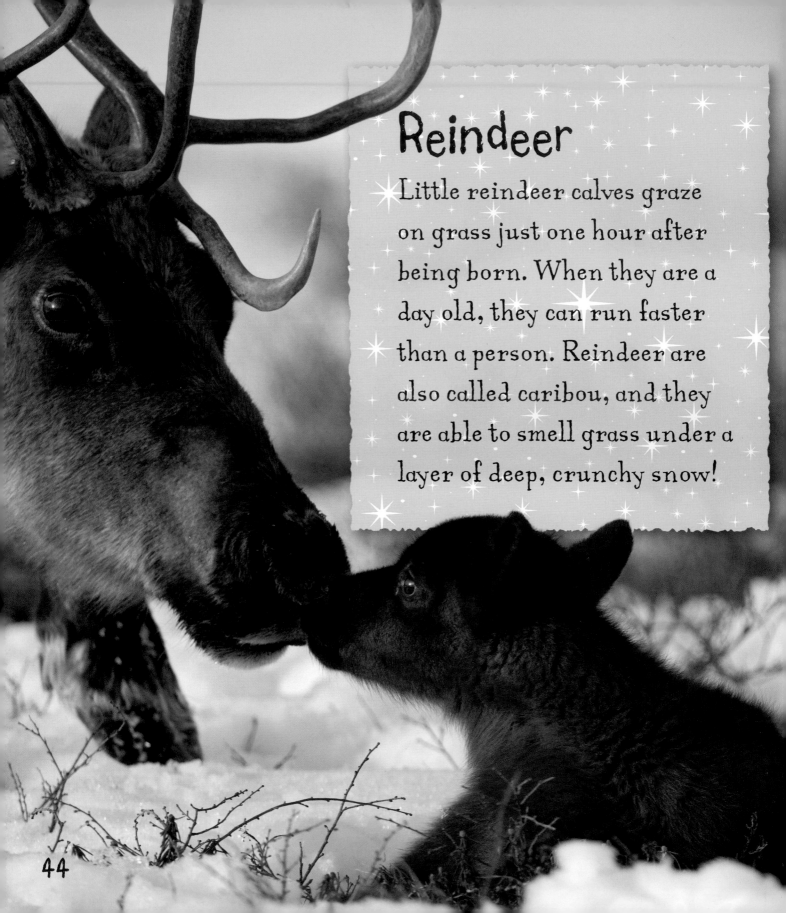

Reindeer

Little reindeer calves graze on grass just one hour after being born. When they are a day old, they can run faster than a person. Reindeer are also called caribou, and they are able to smell grass under a layer of deep, crunchy snow!

44

The snow is melting and a calf must eat plenty to grow big and strong. At the end of summer, it will join its herd on a long journey south to keep out of the worst winter weather.

47

Sea Otter

These pups love to cuddle! They are sea otter babies, and they will stay close to their mum. Sometimes sea otters hold hands. The water is chilly, but sea otters have the thickest fur of any animal in the world.

49

Siberian Tiger

Tigers hunt at night, but in the deep winter they often hunt in the day too. Little cubs love to play-fight as it's a good way to become a great hunter.

50

Mother tigers usually have up to six cubs at a time. The cubs are born blind and helpless, and they need their mum to look after them until they are three years old. She will fight other animals to protect them.

53

Snow Leopard

Very few people have ever seen a snow leopard, and cubs are especially shy. These wild cats live on wintry, windy mountains in Asia. Sleeping snow leopards wrap their tails around themselves like a blanket.

54

Snow Monkey

It's a chilly day, but the water is lovely and warm! There is deep snow lying around, but a baby snow monkey can jump into the hot springs nearby if it gets too cold.

57

Snow monkeys like the snow. The babies even make snowballs just for fun. While the youngsters play, mums and dads soak in the water to keep warm. Snow monkeys are also called Japanese macaques.

Snub-nosed Monkey

The winters are long and harsh where snub-nosed monkeys live. Little babies don't mind too much, as they have lots of fur to keep them warm. They also get snuggly cuddles from their mum, granny and aunts!

Wild Pony

Ponies are small horses. They live on grasslands where they spend the day grazing on plants with the rest of the herd. Baby ponies are called foals and they stay close to mum.

62

Horses and ponies grow fur and a long mane to keep them dry, even in rain and snow. When they get chilly, ponies gallop around, to warm themselves up again!

64